THE WICKED

GENESIS 27:1—28:5, 10, 11 FOR CHILDREN

Written by Yvonne Holloway McCall
Illustrated by Vaccaro Associates

Concordia Publishing House

ARCH Books

© 1972. All rights reserved.
CONCORDIA PUBLISHING HOUSE LTD.,
117/123 GOLDEN LANE, LONDON EC1Y OTL
Printed in England.
ISBN 0-570-06068-0

Jacob was cooking (while Esau hunted)
and thinking of something
of Esau's he wanted.
And so he looked up with a gleam in his eye
as Esau, his brother, came staggering by.
"I'm starved," said Esau,
"I'll die on the spot.
Give me some vegetable stew from the pot."

"O.K.," said Jacob. "We'll make a deal.
You give me your birthright,
I'll give you a meal."
"I promise," said Esau
and swore to the trade.

BUT once — long after the bargain was made —
"Pssst," said their mother,
"Jacob, come here."
And she hissed a message into his ear.

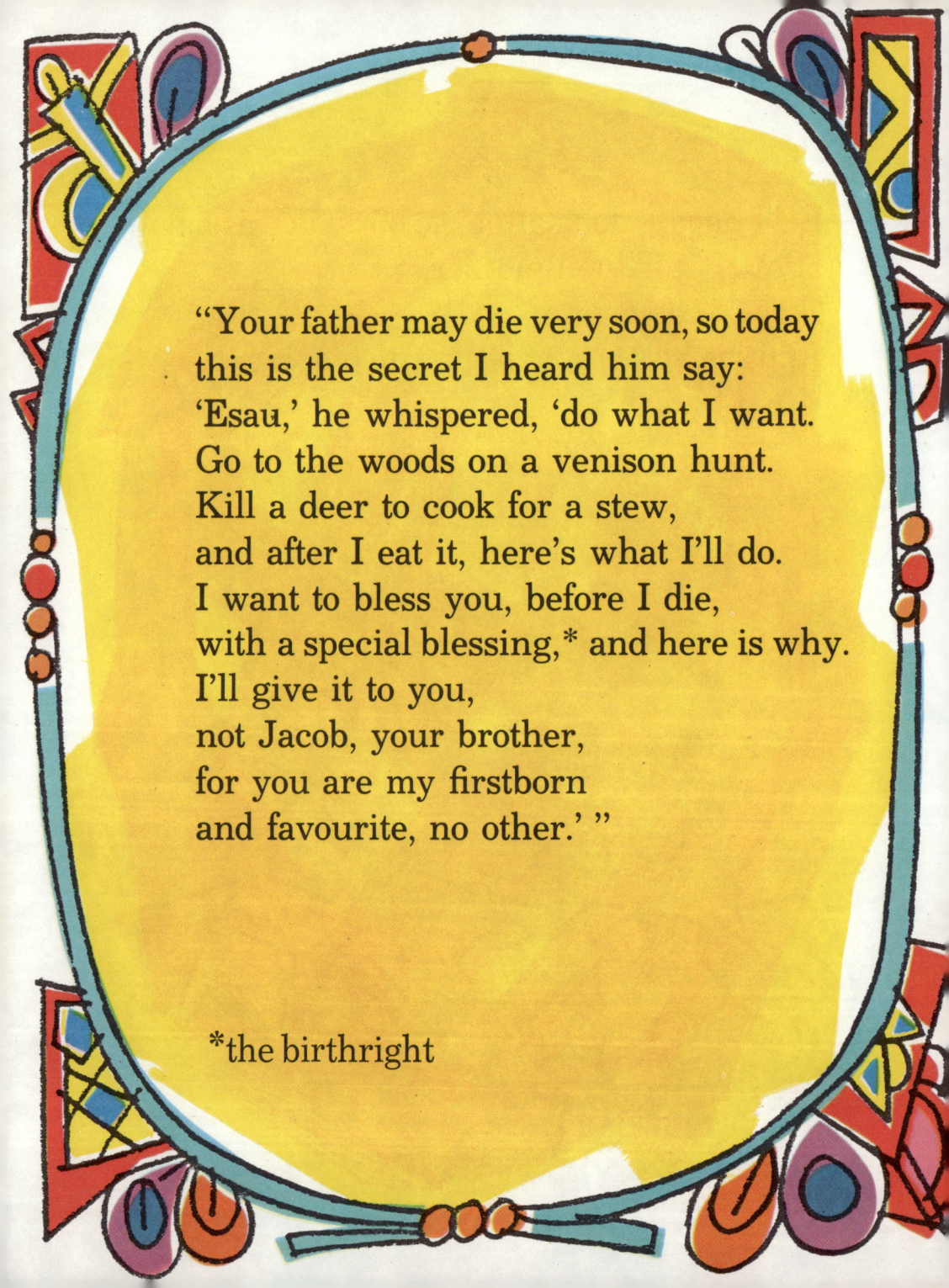

"Your father may die very soon, so today
this is the secret I heard him say:
'Esau,' he whispered, 'do what I want.
Go to the woods on a venison hunt.
Kill a deer to cook for a stew,
and after I eat it, here's what I'll do.
I want to bless you, before I die,
with a special blessing,* and here is why.
I'll give it to you,
not Jacob, your brother,
for you are my firstborn
and favourite, no other.' "

*the birthright

This made Jacob thoroughly mad.
But his mother declared,
"We'll trick your dad!
I've got a grand little plan in my mind,
and I think it will work,
for your father is blind.

"I'll make him some meat
you can take him," she said,
"and he'll think you're Esau
and bless you instead.
Go to our goatherd and bring me a kid.
In fact, bring two." So Jacob did.

"Suppose, when I give him
the meat to eat,
he feels my hands and knows I'm a cheat?
For my brother is hairy, and I am not.
And he'll know the difference,
and then I'll get caught."

But his mother was clever,
and here's what she did.
She put on his hands some skin from a kid.
From Esau's clothes she picked his best
and gave them to Jacob.
And when he was dressed —

"Father," he lied, "I'm Esau, your son. Eat this and bless me as soon as you're done."

Isaac, his father, before very long
frowned, for he knew
that something was wrong.
"Your voice is like Jacob's,"
his father replied.
"Come," he said sternly,
"kneel at my side."

He sniffed, but the scent
of a hunter arose —
the smell of the fields from Esau's clothes.
He stroked the hand that lay on his knee.
It felt very hairy as Esau's would be.

So Jacob was blessed instead of his brother.
And now they were pleased —
he and his mother.

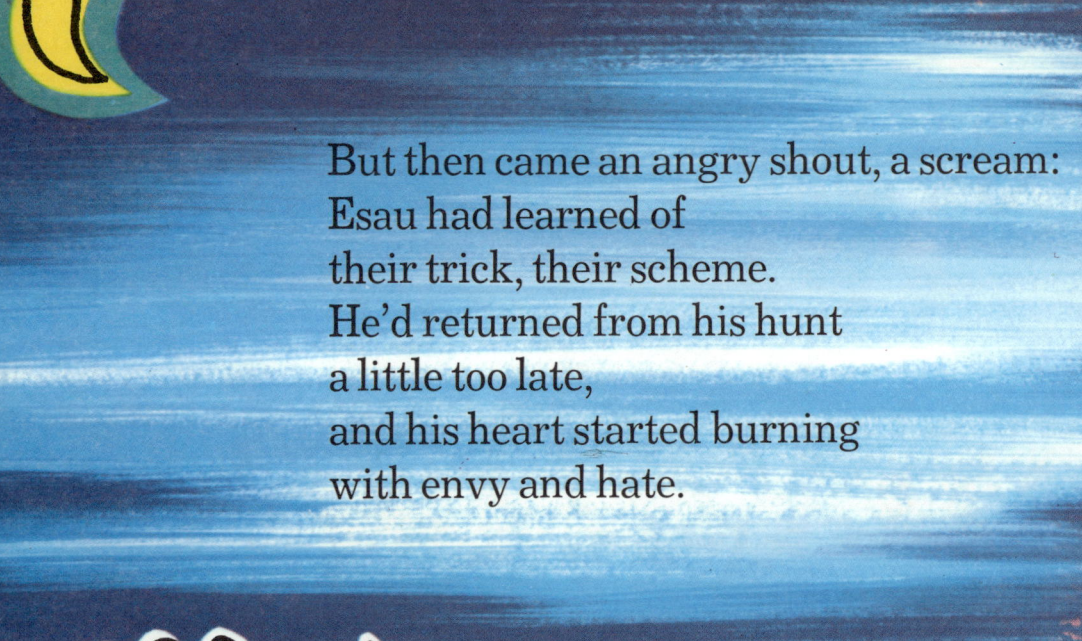

But then came an angry shout, a scream:
Esau had learned of
their trick, their scheme.
He'd returned from his hunt
a little too late,
and his heart started burning
with envy and hate.

And the news reached Jacob one afternoon that Esau was planning to murder him soon.

"Son," cried his mother,
"run for your life.
And while you're away,
you can look for a wife.
In a distant land
your uncle — my brother —
has two lovely daughters.
Choose one or the other."

"Yes, go to your uncle's,"
his father agreed.
"It's time you were married.
It's time indeed."

So Jacob, alone, in the heat of the day quietly packed and sneaked away.

He walked and he ran,
always glancing behind;
the stones bruised his feet,
and the dust made him blind.

With a prayer that God
should pity and keep
homesick poor Jacob,
he lay down to sleep
with no one to hug and no one to fight
and nothing but stones
for pillows at night.

Dear Parents:

Many people are shocked to learn what a treacherous person Jacob was. Jacob! The head of the nation of Israel, to whom the Lord gave the special name of "Israel."

But the Bible is honest, and it shows us how weak and inconsistent even heroes of faith can be.

Here we have an incident from the early life of Jacob, the schemer and deceiver. We cannot approve of his Wicked Trick, even though God used it for good.

Use this story to help your child understand the people in the Bible as real and completely human, just like you and me. They were weak and they made mistakes. Some pretty bad ones too.

But God is loving and forgiving. He is a Father who does not give up on His children but patiently leads them step by step to understand His will and to do it.

Jacob was not blessed for his wicked trick on his brother Esau and his father Isaac. He suffered in many ways for his craftiness. And he himself was the victim of treachery by his uncle Laban and by his own sons.

Have your child imagine what he thinks might happen to Jacob as he runs away from home and from his brother's anger. Ask: What would you do if someone cheated you out of something you wanted? Suppose you were Esau. Suppose you were Jacob. Have you ever done something wrong and then felt bad about it?

THE EDITOR